Chinese Folk Songs

— An anthology of 25 favorites with piano accompaniment

Compiled by Mai Ding

NEW WORLD PRESS
BEIJING, CHINA

ISBN 0-8351-1394-9

First edition   1984

Published by
NEW WORLD PRESS
24 Baiwanzhuang Road, Beijing, China

Printed by
FOREIGN LANGUAGES PRINTING HOUSE
19 West Chegongzhuang Road, Beijing, China

Distributed by
CHINA INTERNATIONAL BOOK TRADING CORPORATION (Guoji Shudian)
P.O. Box 399, Beijing, China

Printed in the People's Republic of China

CONTENTS

Foreword			5
1.	My Flower	Kazak Folk Song Accompaniment by Li Yinghai	7
2.	Mayeela	Kazak Folk Song Accompaniment by Ding Shande	10
3.	Gadamaylin	Inner Mongolian Folk Song Accompaniment by Sang Tong	14
4.	Shepherds' Song	Inner Mongolian Folk Song Accompaniment by Qu Xixian	17
5.	Lan Huahua	Shaanxi Folk Song Accompaniment by Qu Xixian	19
6.	In Praise of the Grasslands	Words and Music by Milchik Arranged by Milchik and Leng An	21
7.	Song of the Mountain Stream	Yunnan Folk Song Accompaniment by Li Yinghai	23
8.	Kangding Love Song	Xikang Folk Song Arranged by Jiang Dingxian	25
9.	Song of the Four Seasons	Qinghai Folk Song Accompaniment by Tang Qijing	29
10.	Love Song of the Grassland	Qinghai Folk Song Accompaniment by Chen Tianhe	33
11.	Jasmine Flower	Jiangsu Folk Song Accompaniment by Shen Wujun	34
12.	Fengyang Flower Drum Song	Fengyang, Anhui Province Han Folk Song Accompaniment by Mai Ding	38

13.	Meeting at the Carnival	Words by Malaqinfu Music by Tong Fu Accompaniment by Tong Zhongliang	40
14.	Song of the Horse Herdsmen	Words and Music by Shi Fu Accompaniment by Sheng Yin	42
15.	The Maid Who Loves to Sing	Words by Jin Zhong Music by Zhu Liqian Accompaniment by Shi Wanchun	44
16.	Riding on the Grasslands	Lyrics by Ma Hanbing Music by Li Juchuan Accompaniment by Deng Erjing	50
17.	Alamuhan	Uygur Folk Song Accompaniment by Li Yinghai	53
18.	Send Me a Single Rose	Uygur Folk Song Arranged by Ge Shunzhong	55
19.	Beauty's Everywhere	Lyrics by Huang Chiyi Music by Dai Yuwu	58
20.	Song of the Great Wall	Lyrics by Zhang Denghuan Music by Tian Guang Accompaniment by Mai Ding	63
21.	The North Wind Blows	Words by He Jingzhi and Ding Yi Music by Zhang Lu and Ma Ke	65
22.	Mountain Song	Accompaniment by Tong Zhongliang	67
23.	The Future of the Countryside Is Bright	Lyrics by Chen Xinhuo Music by Shi Lemeng Accompaniment by Mai Ding	68
24.	The Waves of Gulang Isle	Lyrics by Zhang Li and Hong Shu Music by Zhong Limin	70
25.	Guest from Afar, oh, Won't You Stay a While	Lyrics by Fan Yu Arranged by Mai Ding	72

FOREWORD

Songs naturally play an important role in the world of music, while in the specific context of vocal music, folk songs and songs composed in folk style enjoy universal popularity.

CHINESE FOLK SONGS was conceived to meet the needs of music lovers in China and throughout the rest of the world. For this volume, we have selected such favorites as *Kangding Love Song*, *Song of the Mountain Stream*, and *Shepherds' Song*, all long appreciated by the Chinese people for their beauty, artistry and spiritually uplifting qualities.

This collection includes songs of the Han nationality as well as songs of China's minority nationalities; the vigorous songs of the north and the more gentle songs of the south; and traditional folk songs and songs composed in folk style. All are equally suitable for stage performance or for singing among friends.

Finally, the piano accompaniments provided for each song have been selected and composed with an end to seeking the greatest possible variety in musical styles.

Mai Ding

MY FLOWER

Kazak Folk Song
Accompaniment by Li Yinghai

Allegretto non troppo

Your dear name is music to my ears,
You are like the boundless azure sea,
Your dear name is sweet as flowers of spring,
Though one glance is all we two have shared,

ah!
ah!
ah!
ah!
　　Girl of my dreams one look and
　　I am a seagull ever
　　Slender maiden, take my
　　Your tender eyes have quite

MAYEELA

Kazak Folk Song
Accompaniment by Ding Shande

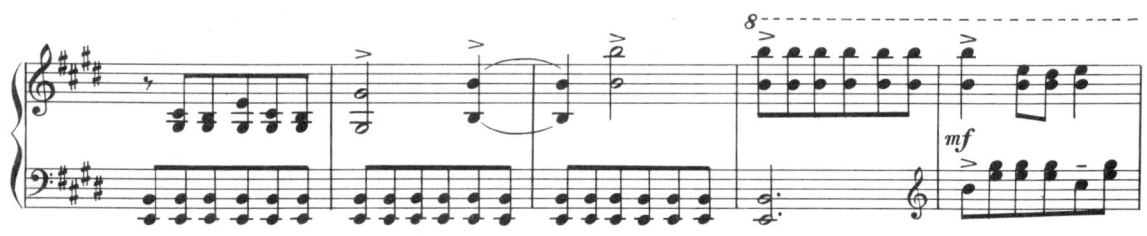

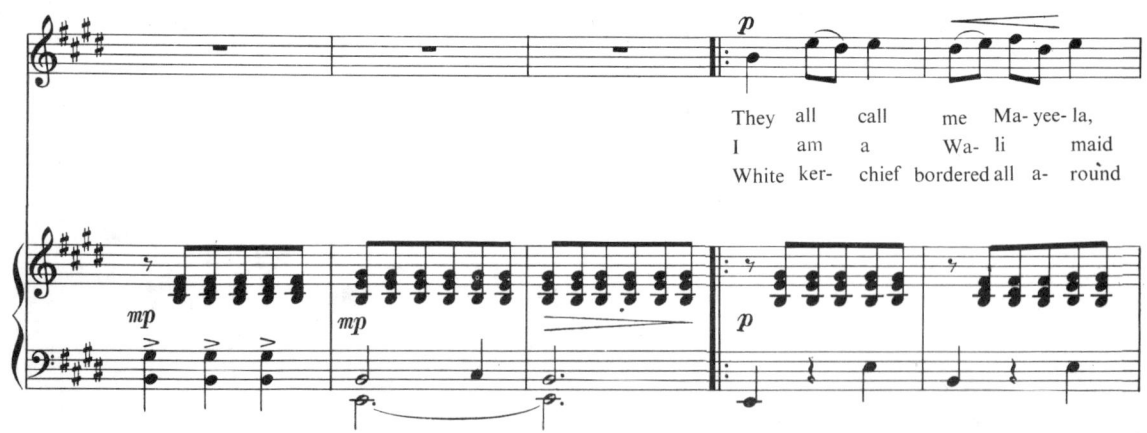

They all call me Ma-yee-la,
I am a Wa-li maid
White ker-chief bordered all a-round

la.

GADAMAYLIN

Inner Mongolian Folk Song
Accompaniment by Sang Tong

SHEPHERDS' SONG

Inner Mongolian Folk Song
Accompaniment by Qu Xixian

LAN HUAHUA

Shaanxi Folk Song
Accompaniment by Qu Xixian

Note: Lan Huahua was a village girl from Gulin County, Shaanxi Province. This song tells of her revolt against feudal marriages in which girls were sold for a large bride-price.

IN PRAISE OF THE GRASSLANDS

Words and Music by Milchik
Arranged by Milchik and Leng An

White clouds scud o'er the clear blue sky,
Should a strang- er ask of me:
Here the peo- ple all love peace.

where the horse herds roam.
What is this place so grand?
All love the plains wild and free.

SONG OF THE MOUNTAIN STREAM

Yunnan Folk Song
Accompaniment by Li Yinghai

KANGDING LOVE SONG

Xikang Folk Song
Arranged by Jiang Dingxian

SONG OF THE FOUR SEASONS

Qinghai Folk Song
Accompaniment by Tang Qijing

Gen- tle spring is here once more,
Au- tumn time is here once more,

nar- cissus flow- ers fair, scent the morn- ing air.
os- man- thus flow- ers bloom, perfume the maid- en's room.

LOVE SONG OF THE GRASSLAND

Qinghai Folk Song
Accompaniment by Chen Tianhe

JASMINE FLOWER

Jiangsu Folk Song
Accompaniment by Shen Wujun

FENGYANG FLOWER DRUM SONG

Fengyang, Anhui Province
Han Folk Song
Accompaniment by Mai Ding

MEETING AT THE CARNIVAL

(From the film *Morning Song of the Grasslands*)

Words by Malaqinfu
Music by Tong Fu
Accompaniment by Tong Zhongliang

THE MAID WHO LOVES TO SING

Words by Jin Zhong
Music by Zhu Liqian
Accompaniment by Shi Wanchun

RIDING ON THE GRASSLANDS

Lyrics by Ma Hanbing
Music by Li Juchuan
Accompaniment by Deng Erjing

ALAMUHAN

Uygur Folk Song
Accompaniment by Li Yinghai

SEND ME A SINGLE ROSE

Uygur Folk Song
Music by Ge Shunzhong

BEAUTY'S EVERYWHERE

Lyrics by Huang Chiyi
Music by Dai Yuwu

SONG OF THE GREAT WALL

MOUNTAIN SONG

(From the film *Third Sister Liu*)

Accompaniment by Tong Zhongliang

THE FUTURE OF THE COUNTRYSIDE IS BRIGHT

Lyrics by Chen Xinhuo
Music by Shi Lemeng
Accompaniment by Mai Ding

Clear, clear the riv- er wa- ter hua la la it flows.
The "four mod-ern-i-za- tions" light our on- ward way.

Makes the fields green and lush, green and lush they grow.
Life is hap- py, hearts are warm, laugh- ter's light and gay.

THE WAVES OF GULANG ISLE

Lyrics by Zhang Li and Hong Shu
Music by Zhong Limin

GUEST FROM AFAR, OH, WON'T YOU STAY A WHILE

Lyrics by Fan Yu
Arranged by Mai Ding

ISBN 0-8351-1394-9

中 国 民 歌 选

麦　丁编

*

新世界出版社出版（北京）
外文印刷厂印刷
中国国际图书贸易总公司发行
（中国国际书店）
中国北京399信箱
1984年第一版
编号：（英）8223—146
00200
8—E—1904P